BODEGA

BODEGA

poems

SU HWANG

MILKWEED EDITIONS

Published 2019 by Milkweed Editions
Printed in the United States of America
Cover design and illustration by Mary Austin Speaker
Author photo by Jeffrey Forston Photography
19 20 21 22 23 5 4 3 2 1
First Edition

Milkweed Editions, an independent nonprofit publisher, gratefully acknowledges
sustaining support from the Alan B. Slifka Foundation and its president, Riva Ariella
Ritvo-Slifka; the Ballard Spahr Foundation; *Copper Nickel*; the Jerome Foundation;
the McKnight Foundation; the National Endowment for the Arts; the National Poetry
Series; the Target Foundation; and other generous contributions from foundations,
corporations, and individuals. Also, this activity is made possible by the voters of
Minnesota through a Minnesota State Arts Board Operating Support grant, thanks to
a legislative appropriation from the arts and cultural heritage fund. For a full listing of
Milkweed Editions supporters, please visit milkweed.org.

Library of Congress Cataloging-in-Publication Data

Names: Hwang, Su, author.
Title: Bodega : poems / Su Hwang.
Description: First edition. | Minneapolis, Minnesota : Milkweed Editions,
    2019. |
Identifiers: LCCN 2019017428 (print) | LCCN 2019021208 (ebook) | ISBN
    9781571319982 (ebook) | ISBN 9781571315243 (pbk. : alk. paper)
Classification: LCC PS3608.W93 (ebook) | LCC PS3608.W93 A6 2019 (print)
    | DDC 811/.6--dc23
LC record available at https://lccn.loc.gov/2019017428

Milkweed Editions is committed to ecological stewardship. We strive to align our book
production practices with this principle, and to reduce the impact of our operations in
the environment. We are a member of the Green Press Initiative, a nonprofit coalition of
publishers, manufacturers, and authors working to protect the world's endangered forests
and conserve natural resources. *Bodega* was printed on acid-free 100% postconsumer-
waste paper by McNaughton & Gunn.

for my parents
    & their parents

&

trees, sacrificed
    for these pages

CONTENTS

사랑하는 엄마 아빠,

일반적인 사랑 편지라고 할 수는 없지만, 이 모든 페이지에 제 애정이 잘 드러나길 하는 마음에 이 편지를 씁니다. 힘들어 보이는 기억도 몇몇 담겨 있어요. 대학원 때 쓰기 시작한 시들이 이런 형태로 나타나리라고, 아니 아예 출판이 될 거라고는 상상도 못 했었어요. 그런데 이 책은 점점 생명을 얻은 듯 커졌고, 저는 마침내 깨달았어요. 부모님 당신이 지난 40년간 겪어온 희생과 어려움을 기록하는 작업은 우리 식구를 넘어서는 일이라는 것과, 이 책을 쓰는 나의 목적은 우리의 이야기를 공동체 의식 속으로 끌어들이는 것이라는 것을요. 이민, 인종, 정체성, 문화동화, 평등, 그리고 그 교묘한 '아메리칸 드림'을 좇는 과정에서 빚어지는 모든 일상적 투쟁에 대해, 또 그로 인한 고통과 압박감이 개인과 가족과 지역사회와 더 나아가 세상에 어떠한 타격을 주는지에 대해 전하고 싶었어요. 사적이면서도 다른 한편으로는 더 큰 한국인 이민 사회의 복잡성, 업적, 그리고 강인함에 대해 말하는 시를 쓰고 싶었고, 그럼으로써 우리 할아버지뿐만 아니라 조상님들을 기리는데 기여하고 싶었어요. 기억 속에 남아 계신 분들과 잊히신 분들 모두요.

말을 삼가는 것이 우리의 개인적 그리고 문화적인 성향인 것 알아요. 하지만 부모님 당신의 삶과 상상도 할 수 없는 희생을 기리기 위해서 꼭 저의 진실을 얘기해야만 했어요. 진실은 아프기도 하고 마주보기 힘든 것이기도 하지만요. 조각난 기억과 편향되고 제한적인 아이의 시선에 대해 깊이 오랜 시간 생각하면서 느낀 것은 이거예요. 복잡한 건 사랑이 아니라 인생이었어요. 당신의 사랑 없이 저와 성재는 있을 수가 없어요. 당신이 매일 새벽같이 일어나 제대로 된 감사도 못 받으며 좁아터진 곳에서 온갖 차별과 폭력의 위협을 받고 일하면서도, 품위와 용기를 유지하며 고됨을 달랠 수 있었던 것은 사랑이 있기 때문이었어요. 제 자유는 당신의 노동이 지불한 댓가라는 것, 알고 있어요. 정말 감사드려요. 이 빚은 영원히 갚을 수 없겠지요.

부모님은 항상 저희를 위해서는 최고를 원하셨어요. 우리가 역할을 바꿨더라면 저는 당신이 평생 하신 일의 몇분의 1이나 할 수 있을지 모르겠어요. 자신보다 저희를 더 사랑해 주셔서, 또 오늘날의 제가 될 수 있도록 희생을 마다하지 않아 주셔서 감사해요. 아이비리그 학교를 가고, 안정적이고 고연봉의 직장을 다니고, 결혼하고 아이를 낳아서 잘 살라는 부모님의 바람을 이뤄드리지 못해서 그저 죄송할 뿐이에요. 그래도 전 제 최고의 인생을 살고 있다는 것, 꼭 알아주셨으면 좋겠어요. 제가 어떤 길을 걸을지 스스로 선택할 힘을 가지게 해 주신 것은 당신께서 제게 주신 가장 큰 선물이에요. 선택한 길이 비록 실수였거나 멀리 돌아가는 길이라고 해도요. 모든 일에는 이유가 있으니까요.

말이라는 건 참 중요한 건데, 언어 상실과 문화적 차이를 겪으면서 아주 단순한 표현이나 단어마저 우리를 피해 갈 때가 있었던 것 같아요. 하지만 이제 드디어 서로 "사랑한다"라고 말할 수 있어서 참 행복해요. 어떻게 말로 옮겨야 하는지 오랫동안 서로 몰랐는데도, 사랑이 뭔지 손수 보여주셔서 감사해요. 제가 진심으로 후회하는 단 하나가 있다면, 한국어를 잃어버려 이 말을 직접 전하지 못하게 된 거예요. 아빠, 저는 아빠 덕분에 꿈으로 가득 차고 방랑을 좋아하는 창의적인 영혼이 됐어요. 엄마, 전 엄마 덕분에 심지 굳고, 완강하고, 흔들림 없고, 맹렬한 전사로 거듭날 수 있었어요. 이 책과 제 삶을 다 부모님 당신께 바칩니다. 두 분 없이는 이 모든 것이 불가능했을 거예요. 두 분은 저의 영웅이자 영감을 주는 존재이고 제 과업의 정신이에요.

언제나 온 사랑을 담아,
수정 드림

translated into Korean by poet Emily Jungmin Yoon

∞

SOMETHING OF A PROVERB ON LUCK
scribbled on Wrigley's gum wrapper

Magic resides
In starfished palms.

Survey its yarns—
The many threads. We are

All blood, guts
& wants: alien

Fauna flooding
Jigsaw geographies.

Clench: peer through
Tendril knot,

To lone spot of light.
Yes, immaculate

Onyx, nacreous shell
Of beetle, budding

Pupa, irised tiger's
Eye—every

Celestial offering:
Borne.

i.

This is the waking landscape
Dream after dream after dream walking away through it
Invisible invisible invisible

—W. S. MERWIN

Manholes hiss secrets. Inside: a transistor radio with foil-tipped antennae sputters the Yankees doubleheader. Top of the third inning: *swwwwwwing and a miss!* A Puerto Rican man sitting behind the counter looks out into the street, picks a scab off his thumb as a little bell rings. Gust of wet heat enters with an elderly Nigerian man wearing a beret & leather vest— trumpet case in one hand & wooden cane in the other—his salt-and-pepper hair gathered into a seahorse. He has a distinctive gait, something between a hop & shuffle. Disappears into the back aisle. The Puerto Rican man hears the suction of the fridge door as the bell rings. A Pakistani man in a maroon turban & brown polyester pants sighs as he wipes his brow, thankful for the arctic blast. Dark circles under his armpits confirm the broken air conditioner that's cost him fares all day. The rookie shortstop hits another fly ball with two men on base for the final out—a collective moan. Pipe organ frolics over the babble as they break for another commercial. Fridge door opens & closes again. The Nigerian man reaches the counter with a peach Snapple & two cans of cat food. The Puerto Rican man punches in the usual numbers: 16 6 32 8 7 25 & hands over three scratchcards. Fistful of change clangs on the laminate counter like cowrie shells: dollar short. The Pakistani man pushes a second rumpled bill over the chaos of coins, signals two with his fingers & a wave. The Puerto Rican man shoos them back into the inferno like his mamá used to—clutching their icy drinks & their money.

Alchemy at the indecent hour; nothing is what it seems. By the by, matchbooks from nameless dives emerge as diminutive epiphanies. Catcalls: customary in a city that never sleeps. Desires braid fury. Each flint is a key to a would-be flame. Flourish of smoke escapes like ribbons pirouetting. Gilded by vanities of youth when sleep seems vulgar, ego flirts with inevitability—the underbelly. Horror a carnival mirror: marbled human distortions.

Instead, imbibe the medicine that we are divine beings worthy of serendipity—peace, at the very least. Jesus, Buddha, Allah, Shiva, Gaia, magical bloom, et cetera—we pray to the same source—the cosmic undertow. Knowing, they say, is half the battle, but when will we practice what we preach? Leave it to us to fashion diurnal disasters.

Matter of fact: nothing here is solid. Not our rickety bones, nor our mortgaged homes. Oxygen, hydrogen, nitrogen, carbon— we are the stuff of magma—starseeds. Perhaps in sleep, we can render ourselves sacred. Quell the notion that some are destined to suffer while others revel in riches. Remember, abundance is found within.

Some call it a kind of verisimilitude to subsist without pleasure— simple pat on the shoulder or a half-hearted embrace when the body rings electric. To know the depths of loneliness, rub two sticks together at the bottom of a murky basin for a spark that may never happen. Unearth the map of storied constellations. Vibe the unknown. Wager that fear is not our common dialect. Xenophobic tendencies only yield calamity. Yellow, black, brown, indigo, crystal, rainbow: such majestic frequencies! Zoom further out to commune with the moon before heralding our extinction.

AN IMMIGRANT'S ELEGY
for my grandmothers

How far do you have to travel to arrive
at dying—they seem to be asking. But you might

as well be alone in this room, its bruised walls & shanty
window looking at nothing—spiked lines of a horizon

to indicate your breathing. Chortle, then a gasp:
running in your mind's field through windswept

dandelions & knee-high grass, blades bristling against
your skin like the needle feeding you—to a clearing

where he kissed you as if for the first time. Your lips
part in memory, a sunken jaw caked with Vaseline,

gaping—desperate to recapture the feeling of flesh
on flesh when you were once essential. You bite

down hard at the finger massaging your barren gums;
your wisp of a face turning a cat's indecipherable grin.

It's decided you still have a little left in you, but there's
no use for such sentiments in the realm of sleep, when

your tongue, tied, weighed down like a bag of stones
cast in a swollen river, writhes with itself. Faces

you do not know or remember are speaking with
their hands—shadowboxing the waning autumn

light. You can only hear the sound of rushing water filling your bed, your ears, your throat, your sopping

mouth—boring deeper among the sea anemones.

FRESH OFF THE BOAT | AN ICONOGRAPHY

i.

Tongue unfurls in ruins, low
& guarded as if each syllable unsheathes
a fresh wound. Severed: foreign bodies
clutch foreign limbs. No place
for proper burials, only
tacit uprisings.

ii.

Wander through deluge / shield / from
gusts of windsong / shingled eaves

rise / dreams are
not yours to be / shared

legacy of no/bodies

iii.

Heft hems craving, atrophies
into opal bone fields where
spring's bounty bursts unshut
to expose new realms.

There's no place like home
There's no place like home
There's no place like home
There's no one place

unmoored: tears glint
like oceans among the weeds.
In winter, sleet melds into
mammoth banks sighing *loss*.

iv.

Accused of siphoning honey from hive, blood thickens then winds
along ravines where tubers are exposed to a certain density. Woe spills
into ceramic pots already splintered & mended—balanced gingerly on
the heads of ancient women climbing steps carved along the lip of
steely mountains.

v.

Family trees reduced
to oral
traditions, cauterized   dead
ends of dendrite filigree:
personalities

of myth, disintegrating
like vapor, apparitions
that whisper: *Don't you dare*
forget

me. Don't forget.

vi.

Wilderness: oh how
it bewilders! Head west
toward the wilting
sun—cardinal
vanishing point.

In darkness,
children morph
into beasts rabid
from diets of artificial
commodities. Trade origin
for sugar: they forget
their given names.

vii.

Ballet of looped
        (y)earnings: mirrored

                Wall: begin
                    & end: end

                        & begin: begin & end:
                                &&&

LATCHKEYS

When headlights cast shadow
puppets against the living
room wall, my brother and I
did our best to keep up
appearances: he'd scurry
to turn off the Nintendo
console while I hung up
on my best friend. He splayed
open his biology textbook, I leapt
to the upright Yamaha to play
the first few notes of "Für Elise":
a perfectly choreographed
intermezzo for our parents, who'd
stagger in from their hour-long
commute, their clothes reeking
of chemicals. They'd nod,
father heading straight
to the backyard to hit
a golf ball on a string
while mother silently made
dinner: rice, kimchi, Spam,
as we three listened
from different corners
of the house
to a tiny white ball
greeting iron.

TO INFINITY & BEYOND

Our Ford Granada was the center
    of my universe: fake wood

        paneled doors, beige interior, piano
            sized hood. Cityscapes whizzed by

like a movie shot from a train
    barreling down wobbly tracks

        ready to fly off the rails. Everything
            stood as entertainment: I spied

dueling squirrels, fleets of buses,
    mothers lulling strollers, swarms of

        pigeons & chess players in the park . . .
        The many ways to keep

from listening to them bicker,
    neither able to yield or to raise

        a white flag as father launched
            the station wagon like a rocket ship—

bricks for feet—burning rubber
    to orbit the diorama of the solar system

        I made for Mr. McGee's science class
        traveling to Styrofoam Venus, Mars,

then back. When fuel ran low, my brother & I'd
      blow fiery breath against rear windows

          then stamp closed hands, draw in toes:
            collage of teeny footprints

of intrepid astronauts doomed
      to hike the craters of the ashen *(One of these*

          days, Alice . . . one of these days, bam,
            zoom, straight to the moon!) & drift

past the deaf expanse of space alone.

ACCUMULATION

Ducked
into nooks
raising force
fields against
spittle
rain to get
off the
hook

    Used
whatever was
convenient,
handy—any
way to
liberate
the gibberish
of anguish

Trickle
down, down
from above
don't make
a sound

    Once:
a hanger
to whip me
good—white
wire morphing
into contours
of birds—
a dove?

1.5 PROOF

Never a punch or slap across the countenance: greatness
    is greater in smashing—force equals exertion against

        the farthest wall. Hypotenuse is more than the sum of its
            parts: pearls of a plate + Heineken emeralds

have a higher volume than the density of their whole.
    Take the square root of ardor then round to the nearest

        positive integer, yielding a hunger that does not exceed
            the mean. Dialed 9-1-1 as we peered through

the keyhole from a dream within a dream while booming
    voices fractured certitude. Their authority as he cowered

        at their feet: a compound fraction. Two white men
            in uniform over an immigrant man + his wife

in fetal positions—neither able to comprehend their simple
    commands. *Get down. Put your hands up. Up! Stay down! I said*

        down! Two children hiding in the closet to devise magic
            carpets—he no longer adding up to an invincible giant—

fractal rage lost in translation. Hands folded in prayer,
    kneeled in a right angle to factor: *(x)* must never happen

        again. Multiply *(y)* into the denominator of exponential
            decay. Divide extraction to posit true values of coveting

        zero = the summation of erasures.

EOMMA

She packed a suitcase—not an immigrant bag the size
of refrigerators, but for a quick getaway. Stuffing
clothes into its slit maw, she tugged at the zipper as if
she were pinching homemade dumplings. *Please, please.*
Begging like spoiled dogs, my brother & I cried for
her to stay. She corralled us inside, muting our sighs,
turned to say this was for the best, we would be okay.
Saranghae. We cringed—we were not the kind of
family that said "I love you" out loud. She reminded
me to set the timer on the rice cooker, then got in her
Ford Tempo—drove away. By dinner, she was back
making kimchi-jjigae. They rowed into the night.
Nothing had changed. Next time she packed a
duffel bag, my brother & I stood as lookout, told
her to never return. We would be fine, this was for the
best—but   she must   not have   been   listening

CORNER STORE STILL | LIFE

Behind rainbow Skittles, Marlboros,
Whatchamacallits—a recessed figure

Pines: her profile scored by fluorescence
Like a knockoff Vermeer. Just as

Antique coins are painstakingly preserved,
She's rendered motionless: boxed in.

Days endless. Hubbub of restive streets
Beyond tchotchkes & plexiglass ricochets

Off walls exalting the departed: framed
First dollar bill, photos of random

Strangers jaundiced with soot & wear.
She, a generation without *proof* of birth—

Not a single memento containing any
Modicum of mirth. Holding her tongue

With a fury untouched—a solitude so great,
She remains mighty in anonymity.

Tangrams of daily trade. Can anyone
Truly inhabit another—how meat

Of the body must be seized then cleaved:
Laid bare to be wolfed down whole

As it's done in the wild.

EXCAVATION

Mom let me lie
on her lap
when she
remembered,
not too spent
after fifteen
hour shifts
to crane
a lamp over
my head,
stretching
my earlobes
like taffy
to get a better
look into
the snail
cave to mine
canals with
a wood pen.
I dozed while
her breath
& naked
bulb warmed
my cheek.
She burrowed
deep. This
was our
only touch
when I let
her study
me—our

binding a
series of tiny
digs.

HAN

1. verb [sojourn; something like a river]

It is occupation
To assume the position: transport,
Heed, baptize, sever, feed.

      Mouth forever an opening, ending.

Ligaments hewed from bone, splinters
Lodged into heels—we're inherently
Refugees. It is elegant

      Carrying only what you need.

Do not mistake hyphenation for lack
Of discipline or vestigial claims as
Surrender. We're told to fear large bodies

      Of water—how easily we are made

To submit. Even in the womb, we seek
Exit strategies, wrestling the murk,
No matter our pigmentation or creed.

      Supremacy is a state

Of inadequate psyches, dizzied by
Desire to accrue more seeds for each
Harvest: futile races to the moon.

      Duality forms confluence: frenzy.

Twin helixes transmute native
Tidal flats—broad & impossibly long;
Our shared carbon footprint

    Made digestible, easier to swallow.

PORTRAIT OF LADYMOTHERING

Rifles through   gigantic   plasticbag in a   redmetal   cart
holdingeverything but what she really   needs   cobblestogether
enough change   crinkled dollarbills   adding up to nothingfast
lets the younger ones   hangon   tire   swingneck   slidearms
seesawknees—splendid   swarm of bees   facing extermination—
wears her gray   like a crown   of daggerthorns   pulls the
smallestones   to her breast   for any mountain   canbe overcome
kisses it better   the temple   anklecheeks   shoulder   bellyfist
saysno in a way   that it sounds like yes—yes   child, yes   you can to
everything   leads by example   having   buriedfathers   mothers
brothers   morebrothers sisters   uncles & aunts   sons   moresons
grandfathers   grandmothers   greatgreat grandfathers   & neighbors
husbands   brokenhearts   unending canon   of terrors   but greets
mymother like a beloved   daughter everysingle   time with a smile
withoutspeaking   the same language   has   forgiven   those
ohsomany!   who have   trespassed   againsther   reminds us daily
we are   thesame   just another   orphan   in the making

AMERICAN SEISMOLOGY
Queensbridge Projects, NYC, 1989

In the hull of our store with an elevated
          counter, I watched my mother rock away
     hours to hawk weaves of braided hair,

water guns, gold chains, Knickerbocker
          wares, AAA batteries behind bulletproof
     glass—walls outfitted with fake

designer apparel. As my father duplicated
          skylines of brass keys, the machine's
     timbre rising above the bass of

souped-up cars, I manned the rusty cash
          register during summer breaks—
     we three waking at dawn to make

the trek below the bridge where struts and
          trusses lanced shadows across the East
     River, high-rises towering like

distant mountain ranges. Out front, prides
          of wise men lingered on milk crates to
     rattle the day's news, rolling

loose tobacco against limp dollar bills
          while children chased on worn Astroturf
     lawns behind wrought iron palisades

with nowhere else to play. Hulking
          concrete monsters lurked above—their
     curtained eyes, barbed teeth

ready to devour heads: *eviscerate*,
              incarcerate! As women, young and old, sat
       on nearby stoops to escape the siren

heat humming aged psalms, they cradled
              cooing newborns to their chests—*please*
       Lord, have mercy!—as bands of white rookie

cops circled a five-block radius hitting
              their nightsticks against accordion metal
       fences, memorizing faces to incarcerate,

eviscerate. I'd count down the minutes
              'til six o'clock when my parents switched off
       the lights, taking stock of these terrible

hierarchies, wages stuffed into the lining
              of their pants, while I idled in the car as
       they locked up—the engine running.

HOPSCOTCH
for Heather, Dana & Natasha

We invented kingdoms in the alley that
        summer—housing projects sandwiched

between a Baptist church & synagogue—
        bricked monstrosities where witches &

hunchbacks surely lived. Daring each other
        to climb imagined steeples, ring the bell,

we squealed in the boxed chase. Blindfolded
        with glee, our fingers covered in chalk like

dried milk—we clapped above our heads in
        unison. Clouds of pixie dust & daylight stars.

When your Mom brought an iced pitcher
        sweating Kool-Aid (*in cherry!*), we pretended

to be vampires—thick as thieves—crushed
        flesh dripping down our chins as the setting

sun drained our powers—beatboxing
        against the humidity. We laughed without

punch lines, holding our sugar-filled bellies,
        lips wide—clown-stained. You called me

silly for wanting my hair braided in rows like
        yours. *No way, José*, you echoed: shiny beads

won't tame such slippery eels! We thought
        ourselves Siamese: yellow & black, black &

yellow—a jolly, three-headed creature forever
        conjoined—not knowing my parents would

flee to where it'd be impossible to revel with
        sisters whose marvel wasn't make-believe.

Hundreds, if not a thousandtimes, driving by Exit 24 on
the L. I. E.—pingponging east then west, swallowing
gulps past cemeteries, never a right on Kissena Blvd.—to
dodge sardined rowhouses with shuttered windows &
furtive basements interring forgottenspirits: nameless
nomads known onlyfor the beating of their hearts
through uneven clapboards   & there, when you
darewake to the bloodmoon flipping a switch to find
roachtapestries   pitterpattering their spindles along
cracked offwhite walls in that awful time of night as
smallscreams   land   into   cupped   hands   with
newfoundwords unknown to your elders probably   still

CONJURE: DAUGHTER

In frilly tutu—pastel like Easter
Eggs—cornflower, seafoam, periwinkle,

Mint—adorable, dainty, fragile. Spinning
Toile doing the cancan down the street

While cradling an infant doll named Daisy
May, her synthetic braids matted with

A smidgen of dirt, sticky toffee. How darling
To be this *darling*. Rerun emblems of girlhood:

Saccharine sweet cheeks like Pink Ladies.
Not the rascal scurrying into imaginary woods

Chasing after starlings & bunny rabbits. *Think*:
More Mary, less Laura Ingalls—beautifully

Dutiful, so mild-mannered! To be picture
Perfect (handmaid in the making) for me

An impossible feat. I was, after all, no violin
Or piano virtuoso, merely third chair at

Flute, zero scholarships to medical school.
Too noncommittal to be goth or punk, just

Riddled with suburban angst, prattling on
The phone behind a locked door with signs

That read: *Knock Before You Enter* & *Private Zone Ahead*. Totally unremarkable. Certainly, progeny

Unworthy of martyrdom—to think, the many
Years I held my poor parents' lives for ransom.

SHOW ME WHERE IT HURTS

I see it before it happens: a lone buck leaps
through scrim of porous brush & smashes

a windshield, headlights flicker like Morse code
in the dark dark dark. Warm steam leaves

the body, hiccupping its final gasps, desperately
clinging to evolution. I see my own breath hover

before tasting blood in the air—heat of twisted
metal wrapped around a tree like some love affair.

A young girl, lily-white & slight, crawls out
of the wreckage & I run to embrace her as if she

were my daughter, but she crosses her arms
into a crucifix as if deflecting a hex—wants nothing

to do with me. Who's watching over you, I ask,
but she cries: *Are we dead yet?*

Drawing near, I coax her with a piece of candy
found in my pocket. No one can refuse a sugar fix.

She's named Alice & I can't help but think
of Wonderland—the privilege of fairy tales,

however surreal or bland, & happy endings teeming
with talking animals in fancy top hats. I rise,

feeling like we spoke for hours, but it was simply
fantasy. This is the only way I escape the world

in free fall, where up is down & down is up,
the rabbit hole pushed inside out. Once upon a time

when I was a teacher, I told my students to never
end a story with characters waking from a dream.

A real cheap trick, I proclaimed, not to resolve any
narratives, disregard the heft of personal histories—

logic without a care. But maybe I was wrong:
Let's make everything a dream.

Keep plots real thin. Because in this world, if I met
a girl named Alice along an unlit lane, she'd be

a brown girl, or a Black girl, or a Native girl &
I'd have to concoct a hoax to have her turn away

from all the roadkill, forget the tear across
her stomach, her intestines spilling—gutted. I'd have

to wrap her in my coat, invite her to show me where
it hurt & she'd wave her little hands above our heads,

screaming: *Everywhere! . . . Everywhere! . . . Everywhere!*

ii.

Tracks follow the heavy beasts
Back to where they huddle, herd.

Hunt: a dance against hunger.
Music: feast and fear.

This island becomes us.

—TRACY K. SMITH

WHEN STREETS ARE PAVED WITH GOLD

Turn a page from the Dead
            Sea divide to memorize
revised prayers—deliver
            unseen deities. Learn to
say *faith* in sundry
            idioms. Or, lift your head
to map the confederacy
            of lies—weight shifting on
bended knee pressed against
            fallow soil. Removed
from points of origin—gritty
            hands clamor for remedy.
Dirt lodged under nails:
            conspiracy of labor & migrant
colonies; camphor winds &
            lonesome concessions.
Martyrdom hemorrhages
            like a failed birth:
we are made to succumb
            through the centuries.
Same old story, like
            unraveling spools
of roses—a maze. So what
            is the meaning of this,
a proxy to youth? Where
            there can be no mercy, no
grace? Hallelujah.
            Amen, amen.

ASSIMILATION BOUQUET

open
  your fist

like a nesting
    flower

picture dahlia,
hyacinth

      roused
in time-lapse

lightning bolts
    captured

      in a bevy
of pickling jars

      cup
calyx

    to leaf
through anther

    & filament
to a part called

stigma,
    & stem

    new replicas
to hang around

36

your neck
like garlands

      & gorge
your cheeks

      full
of anthems

FRESH OFF THE BOAT | FIVE SONNETS

i.

First memory: looking out the window.
Earphones stuttering a litany of vowels
and consonants: *a, aaaaah, an apple.*

Don't think I understood what was really
happening, our maiden flight from Seoul
to an unknown destination: Maryland
then New York City. We went from living

in a brick house with a yard to a storage
room in the back of a dry cleaner's. No
proper shower, just a rusted sink and toilet.

I was barely eight when I kept a photo
of a boy under my pillow—an artifact
of a fading past. Mom found it, ripped
it up, told me to keep my head straight.

ii.

Leaned across the counter, called us *stupid
chinks.* Go back to where you came from:
as if it were that easy. My parents stood like
totems, stone-faced. In defiance, they said
hugj-in, a word for darkness—a distancing.

Fear wedged in everyone's eyes. Listener
and speaker in *both* directions—names
volleyed like capsules of venom. Ache

and anguish hanging like lethal tendrils
in a jungle where the ants don't carry

their dead. I wanted to shout: *Stop it!*
But only mustered a fevered sigh,
holding my brother tight as he cried.
Silence: a fissure. Stalemate: a failure.

iii.

On special occasions, we'd head to Red
Lobster or Sizzler, sit in a vinyl booth,
feel luxurious—pretend we were royalty
for an evening. I loved the shrimp scampi,
my brother always opted for the buffet &
if they could, my parents would've put
kimchi on everything. Whenever they
asked waitresses questions in their broken
English, I'd sulk into my sticky seat—my
cheeks boiling, my claws grappling the air.
Our outings became few and far between.
I'd prove terrible in math. No hope of
getting into Harvard, Princeton, or Yale,
of becoming a doctor or engineer.

iv.

Bulletproof glass is not skin: not porous
nor forgiving. It keeps everything in

and people out, like a pallet of hard ice.
Cache is locked away, a hegemonic set.

He held her at gunpoint, barrel aimed
for the temple. She kept her arms raised

until he, a kid, turned the corner, sprinting
away with a baseball cap, pager, things

made in China, and what was in the register:
a few measly dollars. But this was the price

of doing business in the projects, where we
were trapped inside human cages—binding us

in a strange circus where atoms of haves
and have-nots always forcefully collide.

v.

Summers they'd send us to Korean school,
two brats whining nobody *else* had to study
SAT geometry at overnight camp!

My brother proved an ace at taking tests
so I conspired ways to break a rule or two,
nothing unruly, just idled behind dumpsters
learning best modes to fit in—be non-*other*.
Wishing I looked like Barbie or Nancy Drew,

my slanted eyes always sleuthing for costumes
to obscure my jaundiced skin. A lizard
without proper camouflage is killed in the
wild. I wanted to sever my mother tongue,

regenerate anew, but how could I have known
language is lost when left to rot like a pest.

JESUS

When my mother cries, *Hey Zeus!*
it cues him to resume sweeping. I giggle
picturing the Greek god of marble,
muscle & thunder. His eyes
remain lowered when I ask
where he was born, where he calls
home, as my legs swing below
the counter—the store totally free
of customers. He bridles, suddenly in my
crosshairs: *visible.* Mere sliver of a man.

Tells me in broken English that he
walked a long way, across many borders
(I'm just a child, couldn't possibly fathom).
He misses his mother—smuggled in
clutching her picture. It's been a dozen
years but Jesus knows she is still alive
from the signed trails of Western Union
receipts. He sends her everything,
works two other menial jobs, lives
with several migrant men in Harlem.

Watching him sweep, I peer over at
my mother, whose shoulders are hunched,
stocking shelf after shelf—wasting
away within a five-foot radius, but
our distance seems to span an ocean.
I never ask any real questions, she
never tells me more than I need
to know—having built impenetrable
barriers. Inadvertently locked in
a vow of silence, there is no arguing,

we are *all* rotten to each other.

MIGRATORY PATTERNS

Seasonal transits cued from fixed

    Celestial bodies: asterisms in

        Cahoots etched like horns of a bull, felled

            Steed, reversed ladle, slingshot.

                Herringbone skeins fan across our

                    Beryl dome hunting sustenance.

                        Anything is better. Many perish

                Attempting the trek, but this is rooted

            In their flight: the true nature of

    Sacrifice.

STORE CREDIT

neon pink flashes O-P-E-N: rescue

anemic lumens of mosquito COLONIES glued in

tart metal like UNRIPE persimmon: to bite

the bullet, clamp a *Duracell* BATTERY

or slurp cerulean pools of *TIDE* to

fumigate skeletal traces, *RAID* spray cans

in tobacco spittoons like tea leaves read by *MR.*

CLEAN, his biceps bulging at 2 a.m.: thumbs up

BODEGA

But we have different voices, even in sleep, and our bodies, so alike, are yet so different and the past echoing through our bloodstreams is freighted with different language, different meanings—though in any chronicle of the world we share it could be written with new meaning.

—ADRIENNE RICH

i.

∞

Mrs. Kim sits on a stool behind the register. She spits gently
        on her fingers, bending back the wad of new dollar bills.

She wears a latex glove
        counting along the corners, nice and steady, like the
                hands of an expert surgeon, archer,

                                manicurist?

∞

His name is Raul. When the Kims holler for him, it sounds
    something like *Lewel*. Asians can't seem to roll
        their *R*'s. Raul stocks shelves, mops the floor, breaks down

                        cardboard boxes.

    The Kims talk
to him by pointing to things. To Raul, they are squawking
                        gulls.

            Par favor, par favor.

∞

He insists the regulars call him Jimmy. Some people prefer Jim,
    so to them he's Jim Kim.
        He doesn't look like a Jimmy. A James, maybe.

His real name is Kim Jin Soo, but that's not
                        the sound of integration.

He roams
        the aisles with his arms folded along his lower back,

              a real ahjussi. Or he leans akimbo
by the fruit stand along the curb, watching the city
                      zoom by.

    When Jimmy smokes, he squats like an old woman
        in the fields or a peasant relieving himself
        in the woods.

∞

Where Raul *comes from*, there are tumbleweeds and   an insistent
        heat. His wife and three children also
            remain. Here

    in the land of bounty, he should   never have to be
                 hungry again,

but his stomach feels empty. So many   mouths need feeding.

    It's been six years since he's held his family.

                He tries
          not to think
        of them as he straightens cans

of beans, tuna, tomato sauce

to face
the same way.

∞

Jim Kim daydreams by practicing his golf swing—his one source
of happiness—a real Korean pastime.

Putt, putt. An imaginary ball
on pristine turf.

When he plays twice a year at the community golf course,
he channels Jack Nicklaus in that hideous
green jacket.

∞

Mrs. Kim watches Korean soap operas on a miniature TV
next to the lotto machine,
the one time of day

she treasures. Latexed fingers tap
the counter
like a metronome.

In a past life, she wanted to be a concert
pianist. To beat the doldrums, she hums
the scales
do–re–mi–fa–so–la–ti–do

though she can hardly remember
herself as a little girl.

∞

After his eight-hour shift, Raul naps on the subway to Midtown.
He moonlights as a dishwasher for a chichi
French restaurant. *Mon Amour!*

Two Michelin stars.

Back-of-the-house family meal is usually
stew from leftover fish parts: head, tail, bones.
On a decent night,
spaghetti with mystery meat
sauce out of a vat.

Has no idea what foie gras is, what charcuterie is. A nice bottle of wine

could feed his village for a week. He sleeps
in a basement room
with four other men.

Raul takes out more trash, never mind
he once farmed his own land.

∞

In Korea, Jimmy was a journalist, even traveled to Sydney. He
has a picture to prove it:
standing in front of the leafed
Opera House by the harbor.

But what does that matter now, when he can't even string

a full sentence together. What is the point of language
when it's no longer yours.

Putt, putt.

ii.

∞

A Black man walks in, vanishes into an aisle. Mrs. Kim shoots up
straight—stilled. She couldn't tell

you why she's suspicious—full of dread.

No real memory
of fear—just imagined scenes
propagated by who knows
who or what.
The man cradles a loaf of bread, Luvs
diapers, a carton of milk. He smiles

but all she can do
is glare.

∞

Sandy is in her one proper dress—the bright blue one
that makes her eyes pop.
She can't believe people
donate perfectly fine clothes
to Goodwill. Luckily, it was buried in the $3.99 bin.

You snooze
you lose.

She's afraid the Chinese lady can hear her stomach growl
as she drops cans of tuna into
her backpack, set on the floor.

Sandy peers
    over the shelf—sees the lady watching a Black guy opening
        the refrigerator door.

                  No one ever suspects the young blonde girl
        who cleans up real nice. Suckers.

∞

Joseph is watched—eyes constantly study
                      his design, jerks and strata
    of skin and limbs.

He lives around the corner, takes care of his daughter, was raised by a
single mother, works nights as a security guard, volunteers at the Boys
& Girls Club, sings in a church choir, but

    without the uniform,
        he knows he is as good as   a dead man
                    walking.

∞

Sandy walks up to the Chinese lady at the register, then runs
    her fingers along the packs
                of chewing gum like strings

                on her boyfriend's guitar. She
    can hear herself saying *ching-chong-ching-chong*

        to that new girl in elementary school years ago
                  every now and then.

She picks the Juicy Fruit—throws

a ripped dollar on the counter

for the food weighing her down like a sack of stones.
                    Almost in the clear. If stealing

            could be this easy everywhere.

∞

Joseph stands behind the white girl nervously tapping the counter.
        He knows an addict when he sees one; can't help

            but notice a bruise
                        at the back of her neck, ochre and green

                                    stamps of
                        a choke hold. A man
                should never lay his hand
                on a woman.

iii.

∞

Mrs. Kim hands back change to the white girl in the nice dress.
        She wishes her husband would come back inside
                    instead of staring into space; he could help
        keep an eye on
        the Black man looking at the blonde girl.
                She sees Raul mopping the floor.

        Lewel, Lewel! she barks.
                            Come, come here!
                    Par favor!

WABI-SABI

              to throw
         add
     water   let earth
 slacken   as wheel
     yields   a novel
 perspective
      occupy   discrete
            casts   formed
      by   whims
 of subtle   pressure
            a nudge
      to   expand   necks
 compress   bases
      intersecting
            curve of   hips
      stippled   columns
 funnels   molded
      into   divine
            vessels
         that   can
 be   made
      to   consume
            fire
      then   destroyed
            in   seconds

SESTINA OF KOREATOWN BURNING
LA Riots, 1992; after Patricia Smith

Angels fled the city swathed in glass
milled fine by hammerheaded fists—
weepy palm trees set aflame against
raging stenciled ghosts. Mutinies filmed live
from helicopters soaring above shattered
bodies hurled to the ground.

Flash: brick to head to foreground.
Mess of limbs, sticks and stones, glass
menagerie of bottle swords shattering
skin and bone in a squall of aerial fists.
With no consideration for life,
white men beat a Black man against

asphalt then Black men against
white, thrashing each other to the ground
as the world watched. Flitting lives
of strangers bounded from glass
screens as I pumped my teenage fists
for nonviolent ways to shatter

class and color wars—the shattering
of another *other*. Stop Korean people against
Black people; undo clusters of blustery fists
scorching everything into sooty grounds.
But what did I know about the glassy
nature of people's private lives—

how we do not always honor the living.
Men who looked like my father shattered
after seeing their livelihoods in embers, glass

shards sculpted into pistols, hands against
scowled lips that hit the ground
as if in prayer, pounding fists

like thunder like rain, morphing fists
into bullets. Fearing for our lives,
my parents closed up shop, grounding
themselves to threats that could shatter—
unaware our Black neighbors stood against
our store entrance to prevent glass

from breaking. A chain of fists to shatter:
not all Black and Korean lives were against
each other—grounded amid webbed glass.

REAPPEARING ACTS OF DISAPPEARING COMPLETELY

Through misted window, they don't notice
    us loiter between trellised breaths—

wisterias of neglected tumors slogging
    through the seasons. Strolling along

a beach littered with derelict sand castles,
    we kick turrets with aplomb but they

continue to look beyond the dunes—
    unmoved. Desperation has corrupted

our eyes. Words somehow fade so we strike
    harder, barefisted, yet it merely sounds

like incoming tide riven among the crags.
    Again & again, panes buckle against

knuckles—our throats stuffed with gauze.
    Willing them to turn their gaze, we plant

ourselves within earshot to declare: *You possess*
    a gift, we swear! The kind of muscle

memory to retool desire's scaffolding into
    origami cranes, propel them to soar

on confetti wind & away from scepters of
    the roving, selfish mind—but our voices

are knocked down by the unrelenting waves,
    the seaboard wiped clean: incessant.

HAN

2. noun [tributaries; not necessarily a river]

Philological nesting doll
like chrysanthemum voodoo,

peony kaleidoscope, ginger
root wrought by callous

      archipelagos. Paternal lineage

tended to their orchards,
crushing soured fruit.

      Mother peninsula ravaged

by neighbors from lands
of galloping suns—gorged on

porcelain throats as howling rivers
spilled plasma into oceans.

      Squids bleed ink—so write it.

Tentacles: an oculus army.
White is choice ritual: virtuous

slate to slip into the next realm
devoid of stains, however

      blanched by missionaries.

Such karmic sorrow—thrashing
one's arms like drowning or

immolation at the proverbial stake—
mewing lambs for systematic

       slaughter. This must be kismet:

unbearable lightness of being
a ceaseless flicker—the smolder.

FAULT LINES

Reconstruct the architecture   of youth before

        Muscles petrify to granite   cartilage

           Whittled clean   before clavicles divulge

  Signs of collapse

Nave spine   transom rib cage   apse hips   flesh

        No longer recollects

                leisure   after hoarding

 Pain between joints   even at the site

        Of pleasure   however once

  Plentiful   Ache

Rolls off the tongue like a shamanic chant

        Kettle spits fire

     We blow on barley tea   listening to the same

   Abridged stories   such reveries
        We dare   not speak of

      Our shaky   common ground

THE PRICE OF RICE

Grain to water ratio must be precise or the result
will be *catastrophe*. I let my mother speak

in hyperbole—concessions you allow someone who
survived civil war, someone whose father was taken

by silhouetted men in the dagger of night, someone
who's toiled since the age of ten, someone

who still eats last at the dinner table. Too much
liquid, she tells me, you get porridge: jook—which

sounds eerily similar to *gook*. The ways we must survive
mortal, moral combat. When I'd come down

with a cold, she'd prepare my favorite remedy: congee,
dashes of soy sauce and sesame oil, garnished

with finely chopped scallions. Simple, filling. An entire
meal that fed a mother and her mother fleeing

with three daughters and the eldest son, now
estranged—how a fistful of rice boiled down

with extra water satisfied rumbling bellies amid
rubble mountains, ghost artillery—the peninsula

cut in half by outsiders then left to spar for eternity:
one blind, one cursed; existential, consequential.

My mother wistfully recalls what remains, memory
broken by age and a willing, as I drown my iPhone

in a satchel of abundance. How I used to play, spreading
its stickiness on loose-leaf paper as glue, constructing

hats to pretend I was a nurse mending wounds or
a famous chef summoning feasts. When I first asked

how to prepare the perfect heap of cooked rice, she
casually filled the pot, placed her hand on top as if she

were performing sacrament or taking my temperature,
letting the water crawl between knuckles and wrist.

Eyeballing it. But I wanted exactitude—a basic
math. She used to tease when I had a kernel stuck

on my cheek or held hostage by my hair: *Saving it
for later?* I've never saved anything in my life

when that's all she's ever known, using her body
to carry and shield, cushioning me from every

possible blow—taking it, taking it—so I'd never
have to be intimately acquainted with the same

country of hunger: polishing each granule clean
with spit for a bit of salvation—a pearl.

iii.

First, there was shatter.
Then, aftermath.

Only later and only slowly
We gathered words
Against our loss.

But last was not least,
Last was not least of these.

—GREGORY ORR

DUENDE ESSAYS

for Ray Gonzalez; after Lorca

∞

Plod the entirety of a country in someone else's shoes. Smell of rot.
Women clutch a stranger's child found sobbing along the shoulder
of unmarked forks. Tethered
to nothing—together—they march
out to sea.

∞

Spotted by a murder of crows: mummified figures half-buried
beneath a stand of paloverde trees. Border is a moving finish
line—makeshift shrines are left to comfort spirits at unrest. X
marks the spot to shallow mounds of polished pebbles, flora
halos withered, relinquished rosaries. Sluggish winds whisper:
pluck prickly pears from hosts, split them open
to resurrect hauntings of thirst . . .

∞

Wren's waifish skull leans against a ladder of fishbone; hoary
scales glitter in moonlight. Dainty ships drift in corked
bottles: infinitude air-sealed. Faraway panoramas spellbind
when pain is sieve. Dreaming of utopia & its tall cities—oceans
never sleep.

∞

A poet says there is something alive
about the desert. Blistering childhoods breed
a certain strain of resilience.

Even in perpetual
winter, you carry
that heat with you.

∞

Disembodied legs & headless chests glimpsed from ribbed metal
piles—bodies lean off the rails to trace reflections in the fever
river. Slurred collages: every night dancer is a stranger
grinding darkness—a permanent gloaming.

∞

Weight of sand slips away in frets of hands
like an hourglass; ruched hem of a flamenco dress
is a ripple of waves. Cutout windows in the hull are eyes
fixed to the world, gazing for words printed
in the embers of stars: Gemini, Dorado, Lyra,
Crux, Cassiopeia, Orion, Lynx. Handwritten
books are burned—their spines
coil & char.

∞

. . . woodland creature guards the shrub picked clean
    of berries—waiting for spring.

∞

Federico García Lorca said: "It's power, not a work.
It is a struggle, not a thought. Not in the throat,
climbs up inside you, from the soles of the feet.
Meaning: it is not a question of ability, but of true, living
style, of blood, of the most ancient culture, of spontaneous
creation."

∞

Arched by the heart of a steady
bulb, eyes pinched & narrowed, licking
ends of threads to forge swords,
lancets—spinning miniature wheels
of a vintage Singer, stepping on the treadle
to compose melodies in E minor for angels
stripped of their wings—for remaining

∞

Odyssey
of what can be
carried
on bowed
shoulders. Prayer
is compass &
sail. There's no
turning back.

consider   the absence of a singular   color   albinic flight
from spectral wheel   spun dizzy to   reveal lilac   verbena
hues of   subterranean bruising   white   merely   highlights
the panoply of   others   their other*ness*   in fact   that's just
the way   it goes: farewell   ivory   shale   chalky papyrus
funereal carnations reservoirs   of gypsum dust . bottled
milk   snow leopard bleached   wings pinned   against obsidian
even if to say everything cannot be Sisyphean   absolute

FACE | OFF

After a few nomadic years, we settled
into a split-level house nestled in a cul-de-sac
away from bustling boroughs, but never
far from wraiths of sprawling estates & train
tracks that cleaved privilege & affluence
from our constant state of deprivation.

A latchkey kid—I often stole
away to the basement chock full of vinyl
bags of worn clothes & box skyscrapers
reeking mothballs—my mother an expert
magpie of things already discarded. Built-in
bar next to the boiler, deserted & unused,
became Barbie's mansion: multistoried
cross-sections of elaborate chambers rivaling
any store-bought imitations. Unlike my classmates'
dolls, who had entire Mattel playrooms filled
with glittery toys & miniature Pepto-pink
Corvettes, my Barbie only owned one other
casual outfit—so I made sure Ken engaged
in easy conversation, half-lying
on a couch made from fabric swatches,
mimicking what I saw on *The Young & the Restless*.

In the throat of this hidden cave, I inhabited
whiteness without retribution. No longer
ching-chong-china girl—I, a ravishing blonde
trophy with perfect proportions. Pipe dream:
I wondered what it would be like to strip away
slit eyes—sick of assimilation, the debilitating
task of tireless reinvention. Then came
the right solution: press curling iron

to sculpt a familiar countenance, black magic
marker graffitied over golden tresses. In horrific
absolution, I beheld plastic melting into a gooey mess.
Oh, the glorious stink of burning rubber!

Without pomp or ballyhoo, I buried her
in the backyard by a stand of evergreens,
Ken thrown in for good measure, a pinecone
in lieu of a headstone to lie in peace—forever.

HOSANNA DRY CLEANERS

He spits chemical phlegm into metal
pails with a kind of reptilian vigor
to free the knot of unknown poisons.

Saranghaeyo

A foot to pedal to wheel to needle
stitching hems, mending tears, she pecks
away in a cave lined with cellophane ghosts.

Saranghaeyo

Counting colored pins—make-believe
wampum beads to trade for another
life. Oh God, how have we sinned?

Saranghaeyo

Ironing press shoots scrims of steam,
odorless fumes of mushroom-shaped
fists, salt of their years dissolving into mist,

I shall bury them here.

CANCER

Feet on dashboard, god-awful music blaring from mixed
cassettes, my father let me have my way as he played

chauffeur, never easing his grip on the wheel down straightaways.
Four hours to my college dorm across New Jersey and the Poconos,

up through Scranton to the gulch of Broome County in upstate
New York, not a word passed between us, mile after

mile markers on fence posts, yellow dashes, streaks of trees—
blurred liturgy of autumn, spring. Summer into winter into

summer, ticking off hours that measured the distance as he drove
and I watched the road that held nothing but our widening gulf.

My father taught me willful reticence, folding desire
into cellular spaces. Perhaps one day I will enter this dusty

warehouse filled with neglected boxes, find the one labeled
For My Daughter, and unpack its long-held secrets. For now, I let

him seal their seams with tape, stuff them into corners. Recently
when I visited, he sat across the dinner table as Mom prepared

our holiday meal, both of them aging exponentially like radioactive
particles. Wisp of his former self, barely recognizable, recited

the Lord's Prayer: *Our father in heaven, hallowed be your name,*
your kingdom come, your will be done, on earth as it is in heaven.

They had just taken out his kidney: the half. *Life of*
failure. Suddenly he opened his eyes, looked straight into me,

and said, *I know you. You have a frontier spirit.* Where did he even
get that word: *frontier.* We nodded in agreement, then ate in

silence like we always do, losing our nerve. All I've ever wanted
him to say is: Tell me something. Tell me—everything.

WITNESS MARKS

*If a tree falls in a forest and no one is around to hear it, does it make
a sound?*

phantom   /impressions
          named remnants of intent/ score/
notch/groove/cut
               /smear/dint/blaze
abrasion/stain—evidence of having

          been touched. Labored
                    /over

∞

          dog eat dog of human
          machinations | *oppression*

          obsession

∞

          Horology: art *or* science
          of measuring time. Which is it,
          mechanical art/speculative science?

          Nothing is mutually exclusive in this matrix.

Study near-invisible vestiges
left by human hands meticulously
tracing the unblinking eye of life's
monocle—each suture restores
chimeras of previous lapses.

∞

Driven by hermetic mania to decipher
Desire to leave a signature
Decode geared obscurities—not every
Departure is accurately authenticated

∞

Measure of time is relative, so who gets
to claim the sum of happenstance
on this heaving planet?

It certainly isn't human.

∞

Will there be a world
to lament?

Celebrate?

∞

Toll: what's been squandered   between the span
     of centuries   & seconds

                             without
                   solace   of blueprints set
                                 in stone or put
     into   motion

           ∞

Future generations left
with the question: have we earned

        our keep/held our end

        of the bargain?

           ∞

At least four generations of monarchs
                    make one
annual overwintering migration   if
                  only humans
         possessed this kind
              of genetic

      recall—an inherited map
            instead of slighted myths:

        to live&
    die to live—time& time again

MASTERS OF RE: INVENTION

Burn the midnight oil
to tinker with inventory like
a watchmaker without manuals.

       Tick tick tick of seconds
       recording divots on walls:
       battle of wits, sole mind.

       You: hunt
       without weapons, just your fists
                    pried open.

Aim: survival.
               Mode: warrior.

       Teach a course on *How
       to Detach Fully,* remove
       yourself from notions of
       nobility—imprinted yet
       inchoate in your genes.

You: shape-shifter, agent
of erasure, amateur magician,
       switcher
              of codes—
player in the ultimate con.

FATHERLAND TRIPTYCH
after Robert Hayden & Eduardo C. Corral

i.

Like a bronze statue of a man sitting on a bench,
Unaware of his beauty, he quietly feeds the pigeons.

Blueblack mornings: buzz of 1010 WINS traffic
On AM radio is an odd comfort as he sits in his stall

Like a bronze statue of a man sitting on a bench.

Once stuffed in a truck's undercarriage crossing
Sketchy margins, he runs fingertips over waffled scars.

Unaware of his beauty, he quietly feeds the pigeons.

Engulfed in darkness & exhaust, he foresaw a rocky
Quest from below decks, arms folded over his chest

Like a bronze statue of a man sitting on a bench.

As reapers continue to peck away, he begs for
Deliverance from years negotiated in nightmares.

Unaware of his beauty, he quietly feeds the pigeons
Like a bronze statue of a man sitting on a bench.

ii.

In Seoul, my father was something
of a celebrity: he, the son of a legendary

literary figure who came of age during
the Japanese Occupation, whose chronicles

of plucky children and war-torn soldiers
captivated a battered nation. I learned

this on Wikipedia—my grandfather to me
an unknown entity. When my friends'

parents found out who I was, they welcomed
me into their homes—no longer relegated

to troublemaker, rebel, wayward teenager—
somehow suddenly worthy. "You know

he wrote *Sonagi!*"
they exclaimed, and I would say I'd only heard

of the movie. His funeral in 2000—a veritable
parade—was attended by hundreds of people, even

made headline news. When we recently visited
the museum built in his honor—beyond the ring

of guardian mountains—my father stood
in front of an exhibition with a life-sized photo

of his father: the resemblance uncanny. Talk
about a carbon copy! We glanced into

display cases filled with his collection of pens,
wristwatches, and single-blade razors—though

not a single word lobbed between us. Audio
tours offered in Korean detailed notebook upon

notebook of meticulously scribbled pages:
the torrent of undeniable genius. My uncle,

too, a famous poet and recipient of prestigious
prizes. Some have surmised our art must

be passed down by generation—*in the blood*,
they espouse to our consternation. How

can anyone meet such lofty expectations?

Oftentimes, in the fractured dawning
of night, roused from sleep, I'd peer

down the hallway to hear the clickety-clack
of my father's computer. Beacon: splinter

of light beneath his bedroom door signaling
the flood of promise. Tiptoeing closer, I'd

picture him hunched over—his face illuminated
a neon hue, the zigzag of Hangul

characters taped on the keyboard for easy
reference—as if overcome by a lit fever.

Crouched with ear to the door, I'd be lulled
by the flurry of hurried strokes, but during these

stockpiled years, I've never read any
of his stories. No, not a single word.

iii.

They have
           given
every last

drop
   ounce
bean
   morsel
spot
   speck
fleck
   crumb
shred
   noun
verb

Unless
           they
relinquish
           nothing

Then
           we take
what
we can
get

because
           of this
           will we

ever
          know
how
to return
          in kind

We make
our own
          ends

HAN

3. adjective [ergo, the ego; a river runs through it]

First came hyena howls, high-pitched &
guttural: operatic. Trailed by slamming fists

on wood as glasses & utensils clanked—
momentarily airborne. Childlike rage bubbled

as if from a pressure cooker: a mini eruption.
I listened to them *tsk, tsk,* then guffaw from

the other side of the wall—late-night spectacle
of rehearsed grievances. A woman's voice

shrieked, *Why must you do this again, why?*
in that absurdly histrionic way in the other

language I can no longer speak. That's how
my ear—Americanized & jaded—registered it.

A man retorted with equal fervor (barked
a familiar timbre), making the hair on the back

of my neck stand on end. Art of the swift
crescendo! There, in my childhood bedroom

still painted a cool shade of periwinkle, I
clawed at the sheets as if a rubber mallet

dinged my knee. Reflexivity: something we
unknowingly carry. Didn't realize my parents

had become addicted to watching Korean
soaps online, retiring to bed a little after eight.

Curious how old age can dissolve lifetimes
of turbulence for the sake of a good ritual:

validation via pixel reflection. *Mirror, mirror,*
on the wall, who or what is the unfairest of them all?

Love & misery make for a very fine plotline.

SARANGHAEYO

Love Story, starring Ali MacGraw & Ryan O'Neal, is my mother's favorite American movie. Admittedly, she hasn't seen many American movies. It's your run-of-the-mill romance narrative: poor girl saves rich boy, only to die most tragically (or heroically, however you want to look at it). I try to imagine my mother in 1970—not yet married, fatherless and displaced since the civil war yet brash for the era—nursing an impossible crush to transcend her fate. Three years before the miscarriage, four before I was ripped from her womb—the keloid blade a faithful reminder. Only a couple B&W photographs survive: they are standing at the altar fixed in time—unsmiling, stoic. This in the name of tried-and-true tradition? Still can't figure out what they saw in each other, but maybe it's because she could declare *love means never having to say you're sorry* before any other English phrase, before she knew what it really meant—that love can also turn. Sometimes love is tying a knot in your throat then taking it to the grave. Sometimes it's hoping against hope that a seed will flower into fable—long after we are gone.

LEISURE WORLD
Seal Beach, CA, 2016

Behold: elderly white men gunning golf carts
to the clubhouse to have coffee & pastries

with other solo men—those whose wives
are dead. As much as it makes me grin to see

these motorized thingamajigs, something is dismal
about this place: vibes of easy containment.

How palpably we eventually acquiesce. Abutting
the Pacific, cookie-cutter vistas & ranch-style

homes appear suspect: healthy desert lawns,
shriveled sunflower palms, cliques of garden

gnomes in clandestine banter & the occasional
wind chime tinkling birdsong. An axis seems

permanently off—but maybe I'm not old enough
yet. Recall: *The Truman Show*, the Jim Carrey movie

about a fictionalized world within a fictionalized
world—utopian dystopia unbeknownst to the lone

protagonist—flint of the apocalypse on the tip
of everyone's tongue as empty planes bawl overhead.

Synchronized wails of gulls & alkaline gusts strike
walls the hue of seashells. Outside: strip malls

& naval exoskeletons seize the terrain. We're born
into some form of wreckage. Each turnover:

a burial. This, the one spectacular flaw of human
existence. So haven't they earned permission to fade

in a bubble where everything is a stone's throw
away: basic amenities deemed elaborate luxuries

as if granted membership into some secret society,
even though they've never taken a proper vacation.

Arthritic & near dissolution—savoring freedom paid
in blood, sweat & tears—their version of the good

ole American Dream: this is what I've always wanted.

SUNCHOKE

i.

Never   a green thumb   I can kill
perennials   without much   guilt
allow them   to wilt   slowly   twist
into desiccated rinds   along sooty sills
Certain   plants can   be grown
in a cup of water   no need to pit into
soil   exert any human   will   So I cut
the ends of wens   their transections
a tableau of latticed histories   like centuries
scribed into rings   of gargantuan trees

ii.

I stare   absently   at family portraits   old
frames resting on   the mantle   & wait
for an echo   but ivy   has grown over
unfamiliar faces   braided through
eyes   ears & noses   like flowering
weeds   We each suffer   alone in
tandem   maybe I read this   somewhere
on an engraved placard   on a bench
lost   in the woods   I don't know
what else   to say   about life & love
& guilt   & dying   & loss &   time
Maybe   it'll come   to me   soon

iii.

As I linger   in my Lilliputian kitchen,
whiffs   of rosemary   sumac   & thyme
emerge like a smattering   of rain
Golden rivulets break   through the late
haze of morning   a sudden invitation
Before   suspending root   into liquid
tomb   womb (phantasmagoric starburst
on my palm)   the southerly   prism
shone a galaxy   I trace   the eye   within
an eye within an eye in perfect   concentric
circles & await   its succulent   growth

ACKNOWLEDGMENTS

Many thanks to the editors, editorial assistants, and poetry readers of the following journals where these poems originally appeared, some in previous iterations:

Anomaly: "Eomma" and "Hosanna Dry Cleaners"
Glass: A Journal of Poetry: "Duende Essays"
Jet Fuel Review: "To Infinity & Beyond" and "1.5 Proof"
The Margins: Asian American Writers Workshop: "Face | Off"
Nat. Brut: "Corner Store Still | Life"
Ninth Letter: "Latchkeys"
North Dakota Quarterly: "Show Me Where It Hurts" and "Excavation"
Poetry City: "Sunchoke"
Poets.org: "Immigrant's Elegy," winner of 2014 Academy of American Poets James Wright Prize
Rogue Agent: "Fault Lines"
The Spectacle: "Han," "Conjure: Daughter," "Assimilation Bouquet," and "Jesus"
Tinderbox Poetry Journal: "Cancer"
Water~Stone Review: "The Price of Rice"
Waxwing: "Fresh Off the Boat | An Iconography" and "Fresh Off the Boat | Five Sonnets"
wildness: "When Streets Are Paved with Gold"

∞

There's an entire village I must thank—I certainly wouldn't be here without the love, support, kindness, humor, patience, and generosity of so many beautiful, brilliant souls. Every single person I've had the pleasure of knowing in the many odd jobs I've had or places I've traveled to or lived has contributed to this book, so thank you.

First and foremost, none of this would have been possible without the many sacrifices of my family. My deepest gratitude to my mother Soon-kyun (née 장), father Jin-gyu, and younger brother Jae, as well as family members here, abroad, and in spirit. And immeasurable thanks to Hwang Sun-won and Hwang Tong-gyu for being my literary beacons. I love you all very much—this book is for you.

Mad love and respect for my mentors at the University of Minnesota: Ray Gonzalez, Sugi Ganeshananthan, and Charlie Baxter for their wisdom and guidance when this was just a semblance of a thesis. Also, many thanks to Julie Schumacher, Patricia Hampl, and Holly Vanderhaar for their support during my time in the MFA program. Sincere thanks to visiting poets Jamaal May and Anna Journey for helping to elevate my work in the short time we met. Major shout-outs to my MFA cohort for offering their generous feedback when the book was a hot mess: Mike Alberti, Connor Stratton, Hannah Riddle, Kendra Atleework, Kristin Collier, and Jonathan Damery. Thank you for your brilliance and goodness—I can't wait for your books to grace our world.

The final version of the book wouldn't have happened without the genius and generosity of poet Rick Barot—thank you for challenging me in the best possible ways and for your profound insights—oh what a gift! Endless thanks to the stellar human-poet-editors of Birds, LLC, Matt Rasmussen and Chris Tonelli, whose close reads made this book go from just okay to hella okay! Special thanks to stunning poet Emily Jungmin Yoon for graciously accepting my request to translate the letter to my parents from English to Korean in exchange for nothing—just the currency of poetry love. Also, thank you for being a badass editor to boot, helping me get "Face | Off" to where it is. Super grateful to Jeffrey Forston for spending those hours with me at the Guthrie during a blizzard to take my pictures. Thanks to Italian writer, editor, and translator Alessandra Bava (who I've never met IRL) for including me in a repeating #amazingpoets tweet among poetry giants Patricia Smith, Natalie

Diaz, Kaveh Akbar & co. since September 2017—months before I even had a book contract. Your wild, delightfully random, and quite possibly delusional championing of my work offered me nuggets of hope during the grueling submission process.

Transplanting to the Midwest from the Bay Area in my late thirties to pursue poetry seemed like insanity, but now I realize this was a gift from the universe. Thank you, universe! I feel so incredibly lucky to be part of such a rich and dynamic literary community in the Twin Cities. Thanks to the Loft Literary Center, the Minnesota State Arts Board, and the Jerome Foundation for their investment in my work. I feel blessed to be surrounded by such passionate, kind, talented, generous souls. I wish I could list every single person, but alas. Much love and thanks to the many poets, writers, artists, and activists who inspire me on a daily basis—you know who you are! Special thanks to my Poetry Asylum sister-in-arms Sun Yung Shin, and to David Lawrence Grant, Bao Phi, Michael Kleber-Diggs, D. Allen, Roy Guzmán, my VONA Minneapolis crew, and many others for creating and nurturing inclusive, safe spaces for emerging voices. Countless thanks to Jennifer Bowen Hicks, founder of the Minnesota Prison Writing Workshop, for being a true beacon of integrity, inspiration, and heart. Also, much love to all MPWW instructors, mentors, and students—I'm a better human for knowing you.

Last but not least, before I found poetry as a late bloomer, I was just an aimless, restless pain in the ass. To my patron-saint-guardian-angel friends from New York City to San Francisco to Oz and beyond, who've always offered me places to stay when I rolled into town, or bought me meals when I was a poor grad student, or shot the shit with me about our seemingly impossible dreams, or cooked me exquisite holiday meals, or let me attend your amazing weddings sans gift, or raged against the machine, or spoiled me rotten with boundless generosity over these many years—I will always be grateful. Listed alphabetically: Eumi Ahn, Shahla Bolbolan, Caroline Breitbach, Bill Brewer, Rhadi Bryant, Jane K. Chan, Amy Choi and James

Kim, Molly and Chip Donaldson, Tara Donoghue, Donald Graves, Jamil Hellu, Miki Iwasaki, Joann Kwah, Ben Lai, Grace Lee, Jennifer Lee, Karen Lee, Brian Lemond, Sammy Love, Dana Maiden, Scott McCarthy, Mollie McLaughlin, Kellie and Alex Menendez, Michelle Mokalla, Douglas Oleson, Katie and Phil Penn, Matt Piatt, Laura Prince and Chris McGee, Bithiah Rosales, Philip Ryan, Maria Clara Sanchez and Tim Berkley, Matt Scinto, Jenifer Shriver, Samuel Spurrier, Anna Stellitano, Philip Stelter, John Stevens, Lisa & Kevin Sullivan, John Szot, Robert Szot, Russell Taylor, Lauri Thompson and Kohl Katano, Kevin Thorton, Anna Vallye, Angela Willetts, and everyone else from the Slanted Door, Bull Valley Roadhouse, Fatty Crab, and Range days, as well as the 10 Heron warehouse and Monkeybrains crew. I love you all. Thank you for believing in me before I believed in myself.

And of course, thank you thank you to Daniel Slager and everyone at Milkweed Editions for making my lifelong dream come true! Thank you for taking a chance on this book, and on me. Thank you times infinity to these magical beings who will always be a part of this book regardless of our respective journeys: Mary Austin Speaker, Joanna R. Demkiewicz, Joey McGarvey, Jordan Bascom, Annie Harvieux, Abby Travis, Meagan Bachmayer, Allison Haberstroh, Shannon Blackmer, Daley Farr, and Hans Weyandt. Grateful to copy editor and amazing poet Kate Nuernberger for making the manuscript shine, and to my esteemed group of blurbers, thank you for honoring me with your time, consideration, and luminosity.

And to you, dear reader, thank you!!!

#nooneisillegal #onstolenland #BlackLivesMatter #humansdonotbelongincages #protectMotherEarth #seekpeace #weareone

Born in Seoul, Korea, SU HWANG was raised in New York, then called the Bay Area home before transplanting to the Midwest, where she received her MFA in poetry from the University of Minnesota. Hwang is a recipient of the inaugural Jerome Hill Fellowship in Literature, the Academy of American Poets James Wright Prize, and writer-in-residence fellowships to Dickinson House and Hedgebrook, among others. Her poems have appeared in *Ninth Letter*, *Water~Stone Review*, *Waxwing*, and elsewhere. She teaches creative writing with the Minnesota Prison Writing Workshop and is the cofounder, with Sun Yung Shin, of Poetry Asylum. Hwang currently lives in Minneapolis.

milkweed
editions

Founded as a nonprofit organization in 1980, Milkweed
Editions is an independent publisher. Our mission is to identify,
nurture and publish transformative literature,
and build an engaged community around it.

milkweed.org

Interior design by Mary Austin Speaker
Typeset in Caslon

Adobe Caslon Pro was created by Carol Twombly
for Adobe Systems in 1990. Her design was inspired by
the family of typefaces cut by the celebrated engraver
William Caslon I, whose family foundry served
England with clean, elegant type from the early
Enlightenment through the turn of the
twentieth century.

12/19